Sefirat HaOmer

Count Within Yourself

Count the Omer Family & Adult Coloring Book

Rae Shagalov

Color Your Soul

Adapted from the Teachings of Rav Yitzchak Ginsburgh

These meditations were inspired
by video clips from Rabbi Yitzchak Ginsburgh
available on his Youtube channel (www.youtube.com/innerorg).
These meditations were not seen by Rabbi Ginsburgh and the
author is solely responsible for their contents.

Contact the author or publisher.

E-mail: info@holysparks.com

- For wholesale discounts and bulk discounts for groups and teachers
- To arrange a creative workshop or author event with Rae Shagalov
- For custom calligraphy, workbooks, or journals
- To dedicate a volume in the Joyfully Jewish series in memory or honor of someone special
- Personal coaching for help to elevate your Jewish connection & creativity

LET'S CONNECT!

Facebook.com/soultips

Pinterest.com/holysparks

Twitter.com/holysparks

Youtube.com/holysparksbooks

Instagram.com/holysparks

SIGN UP TO RECEIVE FREE ART, COLORING PAGES
& RAE SHAGALOV'S JOYFULLY JEWISH SOUL TIPS NEWSLETTER!
Go to: WWW.HOLYSPARKS.COM

Printed in the United States of America
First Printing, 2021
978-1-937472-07-8 paperback

Holy Sparks Press
www.holysparks.com

Please do not write or color on Shabbat or Jewish holy days,
as writing and coloring are prohibited by Jewish law on those days.

בס"ד

This is a gift for:

From:

May you be blessed with success and only good things

DEDICATED BY

DR. MARGALIT שתחי' LEADERMAN
in loving memory of her parents
Reb Nison ben Reb Leibel ע"ה
Golda bas Reb Yosef ע"ה
Brody

MAY THEIR NESHAMAS HAVE AN ALIYAH
IN THE SUPERNAL REALMS.

DEDICATED BY

RABBI MORDECHAI HALEVY שיחי' LEADERMAN
in loving memory of his parents
Reb Avroham Volf HaLevy ben Reb Yona HaLevy ע"ה
Tzipporah bas Reb Moshe HaKohen ע"ה
Leaderman

MAY THEIR NESHAMAS HAVE AN ALIYAH
IN THE SUPERNAL REALMS.

❧ HOW TO USE THIS BOOK ❧

Coloring can help you relax into a peaceful and contemplative mood, so for best results, turn off the phone, computer and any other stressful distractions, if you can. Place a piece of cardboard or a few sheets of paper under the page if you are using pens so the ink won't bleed through.

Gather your colored pencils or pens. Flip through the book and choose a page that sparks your interest. Intuitively choose your colors and don't fret if you make a "mistake" or color outside the lines. Just relax and continue, letting your mind wander and enjoy the colors. Being in this relaxed state can help you improve your life and outlook.

When you are in this relaxed state, it is a very good time to think about and speak to G-d, and to contemplate deeply the teachings on the page. It's a wonderful place to be in to think about your life, your family and friends and how you can improve yourself and your relationships. Coloring is a lovely interlude for creatively thinking about a new mitzvah (Divine Commandment) you would like to do, or imagining how you could do a mitzvah more beautifully than ever before.

It's a special time to dream about what the world will be like when Moshiach (the long-awaited Redeemer) comes, G-d willing, very, very soon to usher in Geulah, the great era of peace that we all wait and wish for, when the world will be filled with G-dliness. When you do this, you elevate the act of coloring.

May G-d keep you from all manner of harm and distress and bless the works of your hands with success, in good health, with great joy, and abundant livelihood – and may you always be Joyfully Jewish!

Rae Shagalov

There's a Holy Spark in each of us
that's hidden very well;
when it's revealed, we make our world
a place where G‑d can dwell.

❧ DIRECTIONS FOR COUNTING THE OMER ❧

The Omer is counted every evening after nightfall, from the second night of Passover till the night before Shavuot. It is best to count the Omer, while standing, immediately following the evening prayer. However, one may count at any time throughout the night.

IF YOU FORGET TO COUNT THE OMER AT NIGHT

Count the following day, but without a blessing. On subsequent nights, continue counting with a blessing as usual. The blessing is made only if every day has been counted. if you missed a whole day, say the day's count without the blessing.

THE BLESSING

בָּרוּךְ אַתָּה אַדנָ-י אֱ-לֹהֵינוּ מֶלֶךְ הָעוֹלָם אֲשֶׁר קִדְּשָׁנוּ בְּמִצְוֹתָיו וְצִוָּנוּ עַל סְפִירַת הָעוֹמֶר:

BA-RUCH A-TAH ADO-NAI E-LO-HE-NU ME-LECH HA-OLAM
ASHER KID-E-SHA-NU BE-MITZ-VO-TAV VETZI-VA-NU
AL SEFI-RAT HA-OMER.

Blessed are You, Lord our G-d, King of the Universe,
who has sanctified us with His commandments,
and commanded us concerning the counting of the Omer.

❧ INSERT THE APPROPRIATE DAY'S COUNT ❧

הָרַחֲמָן הוּא יַחֲזִיר לָנוּ עֲבוֹדַת בֵּית הַמִּקְדָּשׁ לִמְקוֹמָהּ, בִּמְהֵרָה בְיָמֵינוּ אָמֵן סֶלָה.

May the Merciful One restore unto us the service of the
Holy Temple to its place, speedily in our days. Amen. Selah.

This page contains sacred texts. Please do not discard.

לַמְנַצֵּחַ בִּנְגִינֹת מִזְמוֹר שִׁיר: אֱלֹהִים יְחָנֵּנוּ וִיבָרְכֵנוּ, יָאֵר פָּנָיו אִתָּנוּ סֶלָה: לָדַעַת בָּאָרֶץ דַּרְכֶּךָ, בְּכָל גּוֹיִם יְשׁוּעָתֶךָ: יוֹדוּךָ עַמִּים אֱלֹהִים, יוֹדוּךָ עַמִּים כֻּלָּם: יִשְׂמְחוּ וִירַנְּנוּ לְאֻמִּים, כִּי תִשְׁפֹּט עַמִּים מִישֹׁר, וּלְאֻמִּים בָּאָרֶץ תַּנְחֵם סֶלָה: יוֹדוּךָ עַמִּים אֱלֹהִים, יוֹדוּךָ עַמִּים כֻּלָּם: אֶרֶץ נָתְנָה יְבוּלָהּ, יְבָרְכֵנוּ אֱלֹהִים אֱלֹהֵינוּ: יְבָרְכֵנוּ אֱלֹהִים, וְיִירְאוּ אוֹתוֹ כָּל אַפְסֵי אָרֶץ:

For the Choirmaster; a song with instrumental music; a Psalm. May G-d be gracious to us and bless us; may He make His countenance shine upon us forever; that Your way be known on earth, Your salvation among all nations. The nations will extol You, O G-d; all the nations will extol You. The nations will rejoice and sing for joy, for You will judge the peoples justly and guide the nations on earth forever. The peoples will extol You, O G-d; all the peoples will extol You, for the earth will have yielded its produce and G-d, our G-d, will bless us. G-d will bless us; and all, from the farthest corners of the earth, shall fear Him.

When one recites the following prayer, visualize (but do not say) the divine names which are spelled by combining the initial letter of each Hebrew word, (as it is printed on the left of each line of the Hebrew text).

אב"ג ית"ץ	אָנָּא, בְּכֹחַ גְּדֻלַּת יְמִינְךָ, תַּתִּיר צְרוּרָה.
קר"ע שט"ן	קַבֵּל רִנַּת עַמְּךָ, שַׂגְּבֵנוּ, טַהֲרֵנוּ, נוֹרָא.
נג"ד יכ"ש	נָא גִבּוֹר, דּוֹרְשֵׁי יִחוּדְךָ, כְּבָבַת שָׁמְרֵם.
בט"ר צת"ג	בָּרְכֵם, טַהֲרֵם, רַחֲמֵי צִדְקָתְךָ תָּמִיד גָּמְלֵם.
חק"ב טנ"ע	חֲסִין קָדוֹשׁ, בְּרוֹב טוּבְךָ נַהֵל עֲדָתֶךָ.
יג"ל פז"ק	יָחִיד, גֵּאֶה, לְעַמְּךָ פְּנֵה, זוֹכְרֵי קְדֻשָּׁתֶךָ.
שק"ו צי"ת	שַׁוְעָתֵנוּ קַבֵּל, וּשְׁמַע צַעֲקָתֵנוּ, יוֹדֵעַ תַּעֲלוּמוֹת.
	בָּרוּךְ שֵׁם כְּבוֹד מַלְכוּתוֹ לְעוֹלָם וָעֶד:

We implore You, by the great power of Your right hand, release the captive. Accept the prayer of Your people; strengthen us, purify us, Awesome One. Mighty One, we beseech You, guard as the apple of the eye those who seek Your Oneness. Bless them, cleanse them; bestow upon them forever Your merciful righteousness. Powerful, Holy One, in Your abounding goodness, guide Your congregation. Only and Exalted One, turn to Your people who are mindful of Your holiness. Accept our supplication and hear our cry, You who knows secret thoughts. Blessed be the name of His glorious majesty forever and ever.

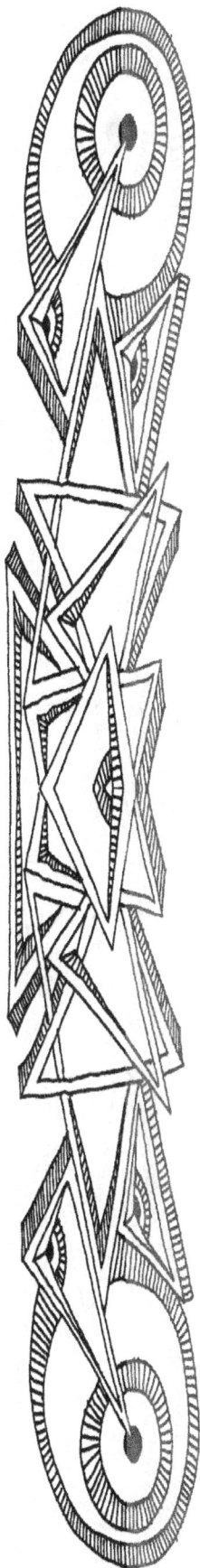

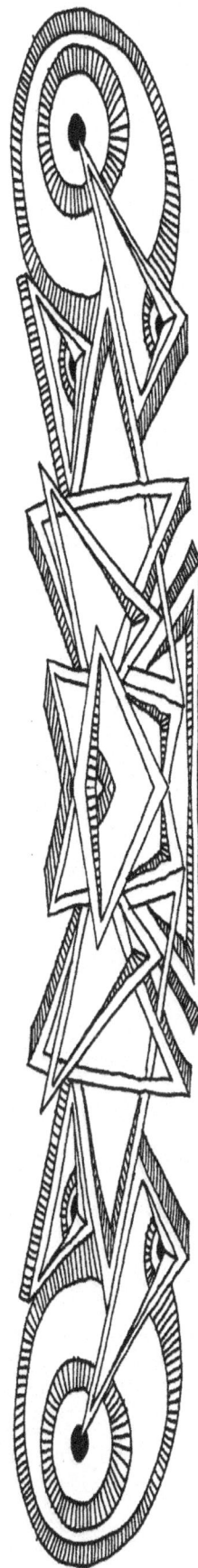

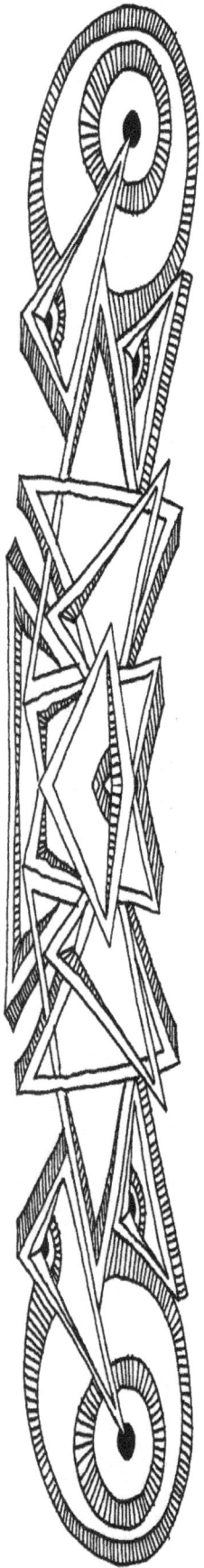

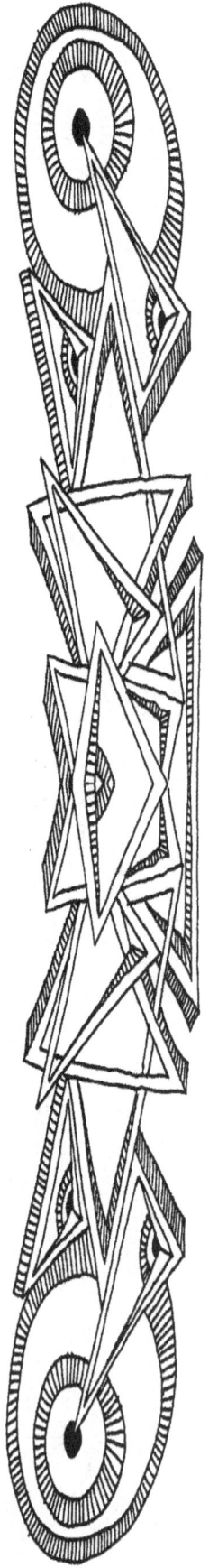

רִבּוֹנוֹ שֶׁל עוֹלָם, אַתָּה צִוִּיתָנוּ עַל יְדֵי מֹשֶׁה עַבְדֶּךָ
לִסְפֹּר סְפִירַת הָעוֹמֶר כְּדֵי לְטַהֲרֵנוּ מִקְּלִפּוֹתֵינוּ
וּמִטֻּמְאוֹתֵינוּ, כְּמוֹ שֶׁכָּתַבְתָּ בְּתוֹרָתֶךָ: וּסְפַרְתֶּם לָכֶם
מִמָּחֳרַת הַשַּׁבָּת מִיּוֹם הֲבִיאֲכֶם אֶת עֹמֶר הַתְּנוּפָה שֶׁבַע
שַׁבָּתוֹת תְּמִימֹת תִּהְיֶינָה, עַד מִמָּחֳרַת הַשַּׁבָּת הַשְּׁבִיעִת
תִּסְפְּרוּ חֲמִשִּׁים יוֹם, כְּדֵי שֶׁיִּטַּהֲרוּ נַפְשׁוֹת עַמְּךָ יִשְׂרָאֵל
מִזֻּהֲמָתָם, וּבְכֵן יְהִי רָצוֹן מִלְּפָנֶיךָ, יְיָ אֱלֹהֵינוּ וֵאלֹהֵי
אֲבוֹתֵינוּ, שֶׁבִּזְכוּת סְפִירַת הָעוֹמֶר שֶׁסָּפַרְתִּי הַיּוֹם, יְתֻקַּן מַה
שֶּׁפָּגַמְתִּי בִּסְפִירָה [Insert the appropriate sefirah]
וְאֶטָּהֵר וְאֶתְקַדֵּשׁ בִּקְדֻשָּׁה שֶׁל מַעְלָה, וְעַל יְדֵי זֶה יֻשְׁפַּע
שֶׁפַע רַב בְּכָל הָעוֹלָמוֹת וּלְתַקֵּן אֶת נַפְשׁוֹתֵינוּ וְרוּחוֹתֵינוּ
וְנִשְׁמוֹתֵינוּ מִכָּל סִיג וּפְגַם וּלְטַהֲרֵנוּ וּלְקַדְּשֵׁנוּ בִּקְדֻשָּׁתְךָ
הָעֶלְיוֹנָה, אָמֵן סֶלָה:

Master of the universe, You have commanded us through Moses
Your servant to count Sefirat Ha-Omer, in order to purify us
from our evil and uncleanness. As You have written in Your
Torah, "You shall count for yourselves from the day following
the day of rest, from the day on which you bring the Omer as a
wave-offering; [the counting] shall be for seven full weeks. Until
the day following the seventh week shall you count fifty days,"
so that the souls of Your people Israel shall be cleansed from
their defilement. And so may it be Your will, Lord our G-d and
G-d of our fathers, that in the merit of the Sefirat
Ha-Omer which I counted today, the blemish that I have caused
in the sefirah [Insert the appropriate sefirah]
be rectified, and may I be purified and sanctified with supernal
holiness. Through this, may abundant bounty come forth into all
worlds. May it rectify our nefesh, ruach and neshamah from
every baseness and blemish, and may it purify and sanctify us
with Your supernal holiness. Amen. Selah.

This page contains sacred texts. Please do not discard.

בס"ד

Count
Within
Yourself

Counting the Omer
Seven Weeks of Change
Count after Nightfall

Nissan 16

1 day of the Omer
Second Night of Passover
Omer of Barley offered in the Temple

הַיּוֹם יוֹם אֶחָד לָעוֹמֶר:

Today is one day of the Omer.

חסד שבחסד

Chesed of Chesed
Lovingkindness of Lovingkindness

Love for the Sake of Love

The first rectified attribute of the soul is to love love,
lovingkindness of lovingkindness.

To love love means that I love the experience,
the feeling of loving, loving another soul.

I realize and I feel
that there is nothing better in life.

This is the actual purpose of life.
There is nothing more pleasurable in life.

This is my satisfaction of life,
to enjoy loving another soul.

חֶסֶד שֶׁבְּחֶסֶד

Chesed of Chesed

Lovingkindness of Lovingkindness

Love for the Sake of Love

Nissan 17

הַיּוֹם שְׁנֵי יָמִים לָעוֹמֶר:

Today is two days of the Omer.

גְבוּרָה שֶׁבְּחֶסֶד

Gevurah of Chesed
Might of Lovingkindness

Love Takes Effort

Sometimes, one has to make an effort to love.
It's not always easy to love another person,
if one feels separation or distance
from him or from his opinions.
But souls have to connect.
Souls have to love souls.
G-d created the world with love,
so we have to create our world with love.
Sometimes it is hard.
We possess the power in our soul
to overcome those feelings of distance
and separation and to embrace,
to take hold, to take strong hold,
of the other in love.

גבורה שבחסד

Gevurah of Chesed

Might of LovingKindness

Love Takes Effort

Nissan 18

3 days of the Omer
Fourth Night of Passover

הַיּוֹם שְׁלֹשָׁה יָמִים לָעוֹמֶר:

Today is three days of the Omer.

תפארת שבחסד

Tiferet of Chesed

Beauty of Lovingkindness

The Harmony of Love

There is beauty in love.
Love is beautiful,
How beautiful,
how splendorous is love!
How harmonious is love.
Beauty means harmony.

Picture yourselves
a loving married couple,
gazing at one another,
like two doves in love.
There is nothing
more beautiful than that.

תפארת שבחסד

Tiferet of Chesed

Beauty of Loving Kindness

The Harmony of Love

4 days of the Omer
Fifth Night of Passover

הַיּוֹם אַרְבָּעָה יָמִים לָעוֹמֶר:

Today is four days of the Omer.

נצח שבחסד
Netzach of Chesed
Victory of Lovingkindness

Controlling Love

We all possess the attribute of love.
G-d created us with love.
But not all of us know how to properly
regulate and control our expression of love,
especially our outward gesture
and expression of love.
Sometimes it can limp, it doesn't walk straight,
the way that we express our love.
We must learn how to properly control
and regulate the love, so that
the love is expressed in a balanced,
stable state of equilibrium.
Then the effect that the love has,
and the power that the love possesses
to unite us, will operate best.

נצח שבחסד

Netzach of Chesed

Victory of Lovingkindness

Controlling Love

Nissan 20

5 days of the Omer
Sixth Night of Passover

הַיּוֹם חֲמִשָּׁה יָמִים לָעוֹמֶר:

Today is five days of the Omer.

הוד שבחסד

Hod of Chesed
Acknowledgement of Loving-kindness

Love Creates Gratitude

One of the most important expressions of love
is giving thanks when someone does you a favor,
or says a good word to you.
You have to express gratitude.
Some people just learn to give thanks,
to express gratitude
as lip service, as good manners.
That's not truly giving thanks.
Giving thanks is perhaps the most
fundamental expression of "I love you."
The more that I love you, the more
that I feel gratitude in my heart
for everything that you have done for me,
and the more I thank you with love and with truth.

הוד שבחסד

Hod of Chesed

Acknowledgement
of Loving-kindness

Love Creates Gratitude

Nissan 21

6 days of the Omer
Seventh Night of Passover

הַיּוֹם שִׁשָּׁה יָמִים לָעוֹמֶר:

Today is six days of the Omer.

יְסוֹד שֶׁבְּחֶסֶד
Yesod of Chesed
Foundation of Loving Kindness

The Bond of Love

Love has the power to establish or
to create a bond, a lasting bond between souls,
a covenant which in all situations
enriches and connects souls together.
Especially in the case of a married couple,
two spouses, who have created an ongoing,
living covenant between themselves,
meaning that even at times when
there are rifts and disagreements,
but the love is always there in the background.
And the love is what always rehabilitates
the relationship, and restrengthens
and reignites the fire, the holy fire
of the bond in love between the two souls.

יסוד שבחסד

Yesod of chesed

Foundation of Lovingkindness

The Bond of Love

Nissan 22

7 days of the Omer
Eighth Night of Passover
Light Yizkor candles

הַיּוֹם שִׁבְעָה יָמִים שֶׁהֵם שָׁבוּעַ אֶחָד לָעוֹמֶר:

Today is seven days, which is one week of the Omer.

מלכות שבחסד
Malchut of chesed
Kingdom of LovingKindness

Love Rules

Love is the most universal law of nature.
G-d created the world with love,
and He rules creation with love.
Each one of us has a spark
of kingship within our souls.
The origin of kingship is the kingdom of love.
We feel attraction, we're pulled to one another.
We gravitate to one another.
We feel affinity with one another.
Love is the king of the universe,
the entire universe, in general,
and also our own personal universe.
The king is love.
Long live the king of the universe, love!

מלכות שבחסד
Malchut of Chesed
Kingdom of Lovingkindness

Love Rules

Nissan 23

8 days of the Omer

הַיּוֹם שְׁמוֹנָה יָמִים שֶׁהֵם שָׁבוּעַ אֶחָד וְיוֹם אֶחָד לָעוֹמֶר:

Today is eight days, which is one week and one day of the Omer.

חֶסֶד שֶׁבִּגְבוּרָה

Chesed of Gevurah
Lovingkindness of Might

Saying No Out of Love

There are things in life
to which one has to say no.
Not everything is yes.
Some things one has to negate.
There are phenomena
which are potentially harmful.
If I really love you I must protect you,
I must save you from negativity.
To save you from negativity,
sometimes I have to have the strength
of character to express negativity, to say no.
To say no is gevurah, in Hebrew, might,
but it's might that comes from a place
that expresses my love for you.

חסד שבגבורה

Chesed of Gevurah

Lovingkindness of Might

Saying No Out of Love

Nissan 24

9 days of the Omer

הַיּוֹם תִּשְׁעָה יָמִים שֶׁהֵם שָׁבוּעַ אֶחָד וּשְׁנֵי יָמִים לָעוֹמֶר:

Today is nine days, which is one week and two days of the Omer.

גבורה שבגבורה
Gevurah of Gevurah
Might of Might

The Courage to Be Strong

G-d created us with the power,
the potential, to be strong if we so desire.
Not everyone wants to bring out that
potential strength that is innate within him.
In order to be strong where we must be strong,
we need the courage of character to be strong.
It's not easy to be strong, but we must be strong.
We must be strong in order to conquer
and to subdue evil, the evil in ourselves,
in our own spiritual world.
Each of us has good attributes
and negative attributes.
We must be able to subdue and conquer
that inner evil, and at the same time,
we must be able to subdue and conquer
the outer evil in the world around us.
We have to be courageous, to be strong.

גבורה שבגבורה

Gevurah of Gevurah

Might of Might

The Courage to Be Strong

Nissan 25

10 days of the Omer

הַיּוֹם עֲשָׂרָה יָמִים שֶׁהֵם שָׁבוּעַ אֶחָד וּשְׁלֹשָׁה יָמִים לָעוֹמֶר:

Today is ten days, which is one week and three days of the Omer.

תפארת שבגבורה
Tiferet of Gevurah
Beauty of Might

Praising Courage

Part of human nature is to admire and to
praise strength, especially the courage
that it takes to be strong in the place
where it's proper to be strong.
Praise and admiration is a response
to the sense of beauty, meaning that there's
something beautiful about being strong.
Each one of us has at least one hero in our lives,
that strong soul who accomplished important
things in life. Helped the world around him
by properly using his strength and his courage
to change things. We have to learn,
we have to be inspired by our hero figure,
to learn from him to be able to also
properly utilize our strength and courage
in a positive and beautiful manner.

תפארת שבגבורה
Tiferet of Gevurah
Beauty of Might

Praising Courage

הַיּוֹם אַחַד עָשָׂר יוֹם שֶׁהֵם שָׁבוּעַ אֶחָד וְאַרְבָּעָה יָמִים לָעוֹמֶר:

Today is eleven days, which is one week and four days of the Omer.

נצח שבגבורה
Netzach of Gevurah
Victory of Might

Regulating Energy

Strength is energy. Every act that we perform,
we perform with varying levels of energy.
Sometimes a person does something,
and he invests in the action too much energy.
Too much energy can result in what is referred to
in kabbalah as the breaking of the vessels.
Sometimes a person acts with too little energy.
Too little energy actually represents a state,
a negative state, which is dissipating one's vitality,
one's innate vitality, one's innate lifeforce.
The ability to control one's energy level in one's actions
is a property of victory, because victory means also
control, the ability to control and to regulate.
So the victory of strength, of might, is the ability
to regulate one's energy level, in all of one's actions.
Not too much, that can result in breaking the vessels,
meaning breaking the body actually, and not too little,
not to dissipate one's innate vitality.

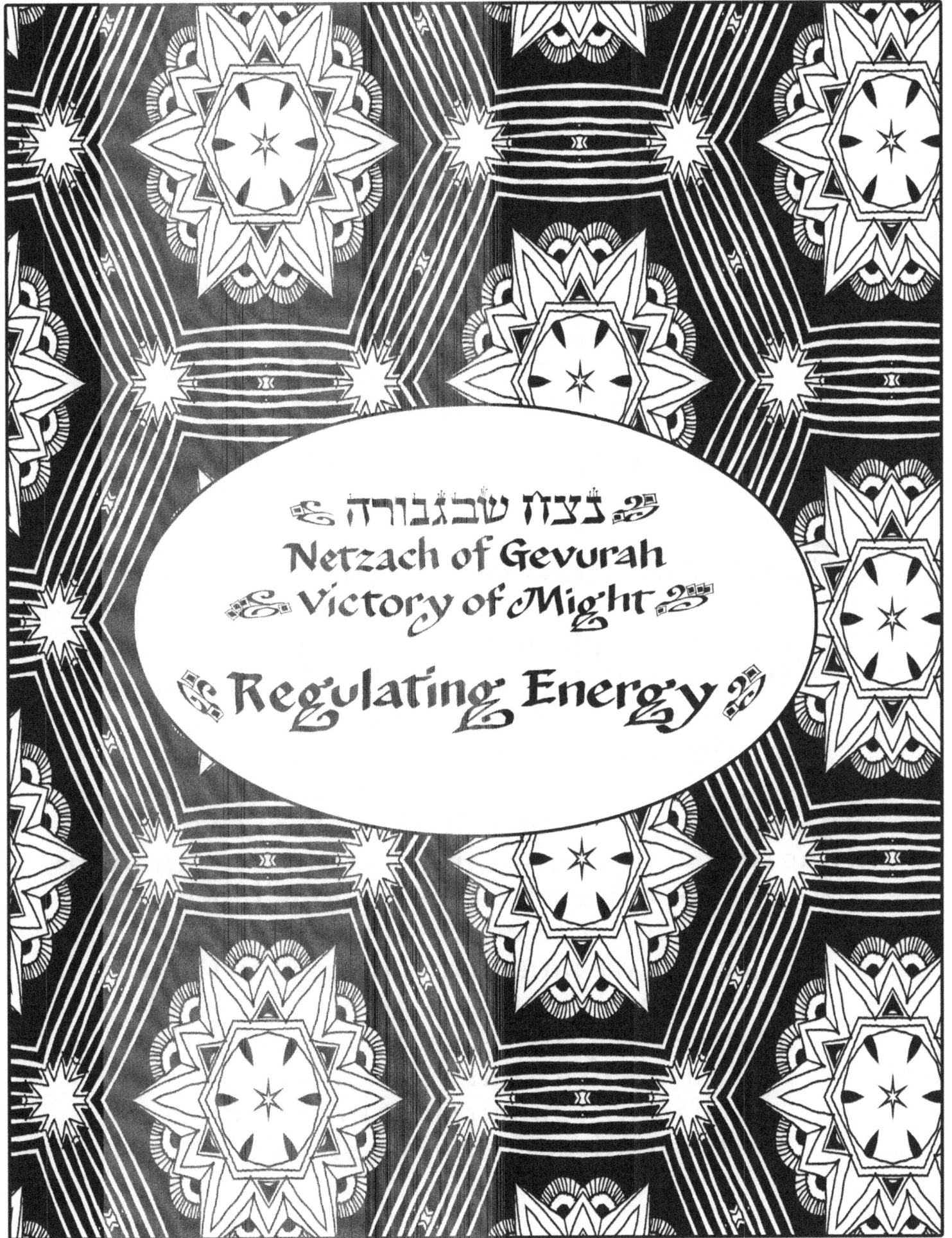

נצח שבגבורה
Netzach of Gevurah
Victory of Might

Regulating Energy

Nissan 27

12 days of the Omer

הַיּוֹם שְׁנֵים עָשָׂר יוֹם שֶׁהֵם שָׁבוּעַ אֶחָד וַחֲמִשָּׁה יָמִים לָעוֹמֶר:

Today is twelve days, which is one week and five days of the Omer.

הוד שבגבורה
Hod of Gevurah
Acknowledgement of Might

Acknowledging our Strength

For many people, in many situations in life,
it's easier to be weak than to be strong.
Sometimes this can even be good.
Sometimes with weakness, one can actually
be strong, meaning that our strength is in
our ability to be weak. But most often to be weak,
means that we are unwilling, unready, to stand up,
to take upon ourselves the responsibility to be
strong, in order to enact some given positive
objective. We must learn to acknowledge
the fact that we are strong and not weak.
I have strength, G-d gives me strength.
I must yearn, and desire, and make
an inner commitment in my soul
to manifest my innate strength.

הוד שבגבורה

Hod of Gevurah

Acknowledgement of Might

Acknowledging our Strength

Nissan 28

13 days of the Omer

הַיּוֹם שְׁלֹשָׁה עָשָׂר יוֹם שֶׁהֵם שָׁבוּעַ אֶחָד וְשִׁשָּׁה יָמִים לָעֹמֶר:

Today is thirteen days, which is one week and six days of the Omer.

יסוד שבגבורה
Yesod of Gevurah
Foundation of Might

Breaking Barriers

Foundation is the power of the soul to create
a covenant, a bond between two souls.
Very often there are barriers which block
two souls from coming together and
connecting, to create that desired bond.
If there's a barrier between two souls,
one must assume great power.
The power of conviction, sometimes even
physical power is necessary to break through
barriers. That power that we have to break
through a barrier with the intention of creating
a true, ongoing eternal bond between
the two of us, that is the foundation of might.
In Hebrew, the foundation of might
is the power that we possess to break
barriers and establish relationship.

יסוד שבגבורה
Yesod of Gevurah
Foundation of Might

Breaking Barriers

הַיּוֹם אַרְבָּעָה עָשָׂר יוֹם שֶׁהֵם שְׁנֵי שָׁבוּעוֹת לָעוֹמֶר:

Today is fourteen days, which is two weeks of the Omer.

מלכות שבגבורה
Malchut of Gevurah
Kingdom of Might

Fullfilling Others' Needs

A king or leader is one upon whom many souls,
many people, depend. Many people look up
to him for material goods to fill their physical
needs, and for spiritual light and inspiration.
A leader is one who knows that he must be able
to give and bestow upon all those that he leads,
everything that they have to receive from him,
whether physical or spiritual.
I have to live up to my responsibility.
This sense of leadership demands great power
and courage. That no matter how many people
are waiting for me or depending on me,
I must have the strength of power to
give them everything that they need.

מלכות שבגבורה

Malchut of Gevurah

Kingdom of Might

Fullfilling Others' Needs

15 days of the Omer

הַיּוֹם חֲמִשָּׁה עָשָׂר יוֹם שֶׁהֵם שְׁנֵי שָׁבוּעוֹת וְיוֹם אֶחָד לָעוֹמֶר:

Today is fifteen days, which is two weeks and one day of the Omer.

⋙ חסד שבתפארת ⋘
Chesed of Tiferet
Lovingkindness of Beauty

⋙ Spiritual Beauty ⋘

People are naturally attracted
and drawn to beauty, and likewise
repulsed by the opposite of beauty.
Our father Jacob fell in love with Rachel
because of her astounding beauty.
Torah says that she had two levels of beauty,
beauty of figure and beauty of appearance,
in physical beauty as well as spiritual beauty,
which reflects itself in the countenance
of the face. In the same way, we must try
to manifest our beauty, to find favor
in the eyes of G-d and the eyes of man,
and to know that beauty attracts.

≈ חסד שבתפארת ≈
Chesed of Tiferet
Lovingkindness of Beauty

≈ Spiritual Beauty ≈

Iyar 1

16 days of the Omer

הַיּוֹם שִׁשָּׁה עָשָׂר יוֹם שֶׁהֵם שְׁנֵי שָׁבוּעוֹת וּשְׁנֵי יָמִים לָעוֹמֶר:

Today is sixteen days, which is two weeks and two days of the Omer.

גבורה שבתפארת
Gevurah of Tiferet
Might of Beauty

Awesome Beauty

There's something magnificent, strong,
and even awesome about beauty.
One can experience weakness
by some beautiful scenery,
the beauty of creation,
and be so inspired,
and become so full of awe
that he actually trembles with joy.
There is a verse that says,
"Serve Hashem with awe and tremble with joy."
This is an experience of true beauty.

גבורה שבתפארת

Gevurah of Tiferet

Might of Beauty

Awesome Beauty

הַיּוֹם שִׁבְעָה עָשָׂר יוֹם שֶׁהֵם שְׁנֵי שָׁבוּעוֹת וּשְׁלֹשָׁה יָמִים לָעוֹמֶר:

Today is seventeen days, which is two weeks and three days of the Omer.

~ תפארת שבתתפארת ~
Tiferet of Tiferet
Beauty of Beauty

~ Truth is Beauty ~

The English poet who said,
"Beauty is truth and truth beauty"
was unknowingly inspired by the deep teachings
of the Kabbalah. The archetypal soul of beauty is
Jacob, who is also referred to as "the pillar of truth."
Beauty and truth are the same. Beauty and truth
are the beauty of beauty, the absolute, essential
state of beauty. That very same poet went on to say
"That is all that ye need know." All one needs to
know in life is that beauty and truth are the same.
This also is unknowingly inspired by Kabbalah.
The inner soul of beauty and truth is knowledge,
the level of daat, of knowledge in the soul.
The essential knowledge of the soul is to know this:
"Beauty is truth, truth beauty--that is all
Ye know on earth, and all ye need to know"
(John Keats, "Ode on a Grecian Urn")

תפארת שבתפארת

Tiferet of Tiferet

Beauty of Beauty

Truth is Beauty

Iyar 3

18 days of the Omer

הַיּוֹם שְׁמוֹנָה עָשָׂר יוֹם שֶׁהֵם שְׁנֵי שָׁבוּעוֹת וְאַרְבָּעָה יָמִים לָעוֹמֶר:

Today is eighteen days, which is two weeks and four days of the Omer.

נצח שבתפארת

Netzach of Tiferet
Victory of Beauty

Eternal Beauty

Beauty is eternal.
It lives on. It never ceases.
The opposite of beauty,
something which is ugly, ceases.
But beauty lives on.
Not only does beauty live on,
but beauty gives birth.
The most beautiful thing in the world is
to do a good deed, a ma'aseh tov (a good deed)
If a person does a good deed,
one good deed gives rise to another,
and then another good deed.
In a good deed, there is the power of infinity,
the power to continue to bear offspring,
one after the other.
This is the eternity of beauty.

נצח שבתפארת

Netzach of Tiferet

Victory of Beauty

Eternal Beauty

Iyar 4

19 days of the Omer

הַיּוֹם תִּשְׁעָה עָשָׂר יוֹם שֶׁהֵם שְׁנֵי שָׁבוּעוֹת וַחֲמִשָּׁה יָמִים לָעוֹמֶר:

Today is nineteen days, which is two weeks and five days of the Omer.

❧ הוד שבתפארת ☙

Hod of Tiferet
Acknowledgement of Beauty

❧ Hidden Beauty ☙

Beauty is not always obvious to the naked eye.
Often one must contemplate an object
in order to see its beauty.
One must first acknowledge
that there is beauty there to find,
in order to seek, to search for the beauty.
Most often, beauty is symmetric, but often
beauty can also entail a point of asymmetry,
That's what makes it beautiful,
like a dimple in the face.
First we must believe that there is inherent
beauty in everything that G-d created in the
world, for His glory, to manifest His beauty.
And if we contemplate and meditate,
we can find the point of beauty in everything,
whether symmetric, or sometimes asymmetric.

הוד שבתפארת

Hod of Tiferet

Acknowledgement of Beauty

Hidden Beauty

Iyar 5

20 days of the Omer

הַיּוֹם עֶשְׂרִים יוֹם שֶׁהֵם שְׁנֵי שָׁבוּעוֹת וְשִׁשָּׁה יָמִים לָעוֹמֶר:

Today is twenty days, which is two weeks and six days of the Omer.

יסוד שבתפארת

Yesod of Tiferet
Foundation of Beauty

The Bond and the Beautiful

Beauty seeks beauty
in order to connect to beauty.
One beautiful object, or beautiful soul,
wants to marry another beautiful object
or beautiful soul. This is a law of nature,
that beauty looks for beauty.
As we said, sometimes we must contemplate
in depth, an object to manifest its beauty.
Sometimes there is a barrier that prevents
our eye from initially observing and seeing
the beauty. We must have the power and the
desire of the soul to connect together, with the
knowledge that the common denominator
of everything that G-d Almighty created
in the world is beauty, and that's what
connects two objects or souls together.

יסוד שבתפארת

Yesod of Tiferet

Foundation of Beauty

The Bond and the Beautiful

Iyar 6

21 days of the Omer

הַיּוֹם אֶחָד וְעֶשְׂרִים יוֹם שֶׁהֵם שְׁלֹשָׁה שָׁבוּעוֹת לָעוֹמֶר:

Today is twenty-one days, which is three weeks of the Omer.

מלכות שבתתפארת
Malchut of Tiferet
Kingdom of Beauty

Holy Charisma

Everyone is a king or a leader
in his own domain.
He must know that he is looked up to,
to lead, and looked up to with eyes
that are searching for beauty,
for his beauty, the beauty of leadership.
A true leader has charisma.
He is charismatic. People want that.
That's what they seek in a true leader.
Each one of us has that charisma
within our souls.
May Hashem, G-d Almighty, help us
to reveal our innate, positive, holy charisma.

מלכות שבתתפארת

Malchut of Tiferet

Kingdom of Beauty

Holy Charisma

הַיוֹם שְׁנַיִם וְעֶשְׂרִים יוֹם שֶׁהֵם שְׁלֹשָׁה שָׁבוּעוֹת וְיוֹם אֶחָד לָעוֹמֶר:

Today is twenty-two days, which is three weeks and one day of the Omer.

חסד שבנצח
Chesed of Netzach
Lovingkindness of Victory

Success from on High

People love to win.
The world is full of games.
Some games are just for fun,
some games are real.
Some games count in life.
If you're the winner, so that's great.
You love to win. Even if you're not a winner,
but you observe a game where there's a winner
and a loser, one is always drawn to identify
with the winner . To win is to succeed in life.
Success comes from God. We all know that
that which we are naturally drawn to, to win,
to succeed, is a power that we receive
from on High, from the Creator of the universe.

חסד שבנצח

Chesed of Netzach

Lovingkindness of Victory

Success from on High

הַיּוֹם שְׁלֹשָׁה וְעֶשְׂרִים יוֹם שֶׁהֵם שְׁלֹשָׁה שָׁבוּעוֹת וּשְׁנֵי יָמִים לָעוֹמֶר:

Today is 23 days, which is three weeks and two days of the Omer.

גבורה שבנצח
Gevurah of Netzach
Might of Victory

Playing by the Rules

People fight to win.
They exert great strength
in order to win the game.
Every game has its rules.
When one fights to win,
one must channel his strength
in accordance to the rules.
The rules are there for the good.
If one puts all one's strength
into following the rules of the game,
then he will succeed and win, in justice.

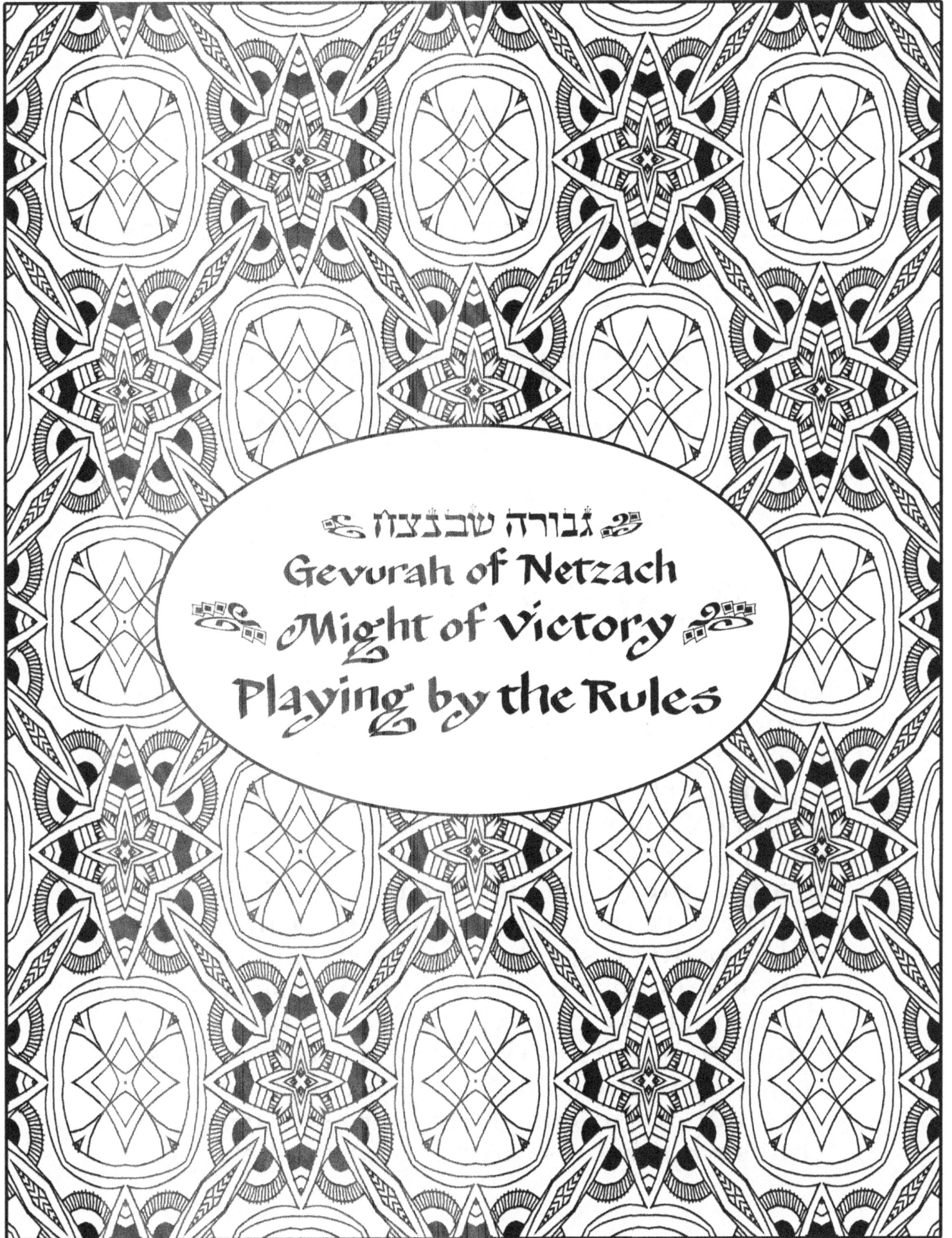

גבורה שבנצח
Gevurah of Netzach
Might of victory
Playing by the Rules

Iyar 9

24 days of the Omer

הַיּוֹם אַרְבָּעָה וְעֶשְׂרִים יוֹם שֶׁהֵם שְׁלֹשָׁה שָׁבוּעוֹת וּשְׁלֹשָׁה יָמִים לָעֹמֶר:

Today is 24 days, which is three weeks and three days of the Omer.

❧ תפארת שבנצח ❧
Tiferet of Netzach
Beauty of Victory
Beauty of Contest

The beauty of playing a game in which there is a winner and a loser is, as the saying goes, it takes two to tango. One must see that both players of the game participate in harmony, and that they properly follow the rules of the game. And so, indeed, each of the two players must show respect, absorb, and experience the beauty of the other, that they are two voices. The winner must, in the end, give due respect to the loser, and obviously the loser must also acknowledge and see the beauty in the winner. We can experience the fact that we're actually partners in the game, even though we're fighting in the game. Each one wants to win, but at the same time we're partners. That's what brings out the beauty of the game.

תפארת שבנצח

Tiferet of Netzach

Beauty of victory

Beauty of Contest

Iyar 10

25 days of the Omer

הַיּוֹם חֲמִשָּׁה וְעֶשְׂרִים יוֹם שֶׁהֵם שְׁלֹשָׁה שָׁבוּעוֹת וְאַרְבָּעָה יָמִים לָעוֹמֶר:

Today is 25 days, which is three weeks and four days of the Omer.

◆ נצח שבנצח ◆
Netzach of Netzach
◆ Victory of Victory ◆

Holy Ambition

To win is to succeed in life. In order to succeed, one must take initiative, one must be ambitious. Sometimes, to be ambitious and to take initiative is ego, just an expression of ego. But the truth is that one must learn how to take initiative and be ambitious, to stand up to the challenge. One needs to take upon oneself new challenges, and to love challenges, knowing all the time that the power to succeed ultimately comes from Hashem, that He is the One and the only One that gives me the power to succeed. But, He gives me the power to succeed when He wants me to stand up to the challenge and take the initiative and be ambitious.

נצח שבנצח

Netzach of Netzach

Victory of Victory

Holy Ambition

Iyar 11

26 days of the Omer

הַיּוֹם שִׁשָּׁה וְעֶשְׂרִים יוֹם שֶׁהֵם שְׁלֹשָׁה שָׁבוּעוֹת וַחֲמִשָּׁה יָמִים לָעוֹמֶר:

Today is 26 days, which is three weeks and five days of the Omer.

הוד שבנצח

Hod of Netzach

Acknowledgement of victory

Remembering a Forgotten Soul

One of the central truths that we must acknowledge
and believe in, is the 13th principle of our faith, the faith
in the resurrection, that the dead will return to life,
and that life will ultimately be victorious over death.
We will return from the grave, from oblivion,
and live on forever. Death means a forgotten soul.
The souls continue to exist, but some souls are
remembered, some souls are forgotten. Resurrection is a
forgotten soul returning to the forefront of our memory,
returning out of apparent oblivion. What does this mean
for me? A forgotten soul can be a part of my self. It can be
a forgotten previous incarnation. It can be a traumatic
experience in my life that I have repressed deep into my
subconscious. Resurrection and acknowledging
resurrection, which is the acknowledgement of victory
and eternity, means that all those forgotten lost souls
and sparks will return and live on forever.

הוד שבנצח

Hod of Netzach

Acknowledgement of Victory

Remembering Forgotten Soul

הַיּוֹם שִׁבְעָה וְעֶשְׂרִים יוֹם שֶׁהֵם שְׁלֹשָׁה שָׁבוּעוֹת וְשִׁשָּׁה יָמִים לָעוֹמֶר:

Today is 27 days, which is three weeks and six days of the Omer.

יסוד שבנצח

Yesod of Netzach

Foundation of Victory

Self-Fulfilment

Each of us has our goals in life.
When we merit to achieve and accomplish
our objectives, our goals, we become full of
happiness, the happiness of self-fulfillment.
Self-fulfillment is a very essential
experience and property of the soul.
True self-fulfillment, itself is creating a bond,
a covenant, with the source of our success.
As we have explained, the source of our success
is G-d. He gives us the power to succeed in life,
that happiness that we have, which is the
absolute contentment of self-fulfillment.
I have accomplished my mission on earth,
as G-d sent me here. There is no greater bond
to G-d than the happiness of self fulfillment.

יסוד שבנצח

Yesod of Netzach
Foundation of Victory
Self-Fulfilment

הַיוֹם שְׁמוֹנָה וְעֶשְׂרִים יוֹם שֶׁהֵם אַרְבָּעָה שָׁבוּעוֹת לָעוֹמֶר:

Today is 28 days, which is four weeks of the Omer.

֍ מלכות שבנצח ֍
Malchut of Netzach
Kingdom of Victory

King's War

The king as the leader
will expend all of his resources
to win his wars.
What are the wars of the king
for which he will give
everything to succeed?
The wars of the king
are the wars
of light over darkness.

מלכות שבנצח

Malchut of Netzach
Kingdom of Victory

King's War

Iyar 14

29 days of the Omer

הַיּוֹם תִּשְׁעָה וְעֶשְׂרִים יוֹם שֶׁהֵם אַרְבָּעָה שָׁבוּעוֹת וְיוֹם אֶחָד לָעוֹמֶר:

Today is 29 days, which is four weeks and one day of the Omer.

חסד שבהוד
Chesed of Hod
Lovingkindness of Acknowledgement

Making Room

I acknowledge
your presence
in my life,
by giving you
full space to act freely.
In this way
I can relate to you in love,
you can relate to me in love.
We must learn how to give space,
one to the other,
in order to properly,
in a balanced way,
express our love,
one to the other.

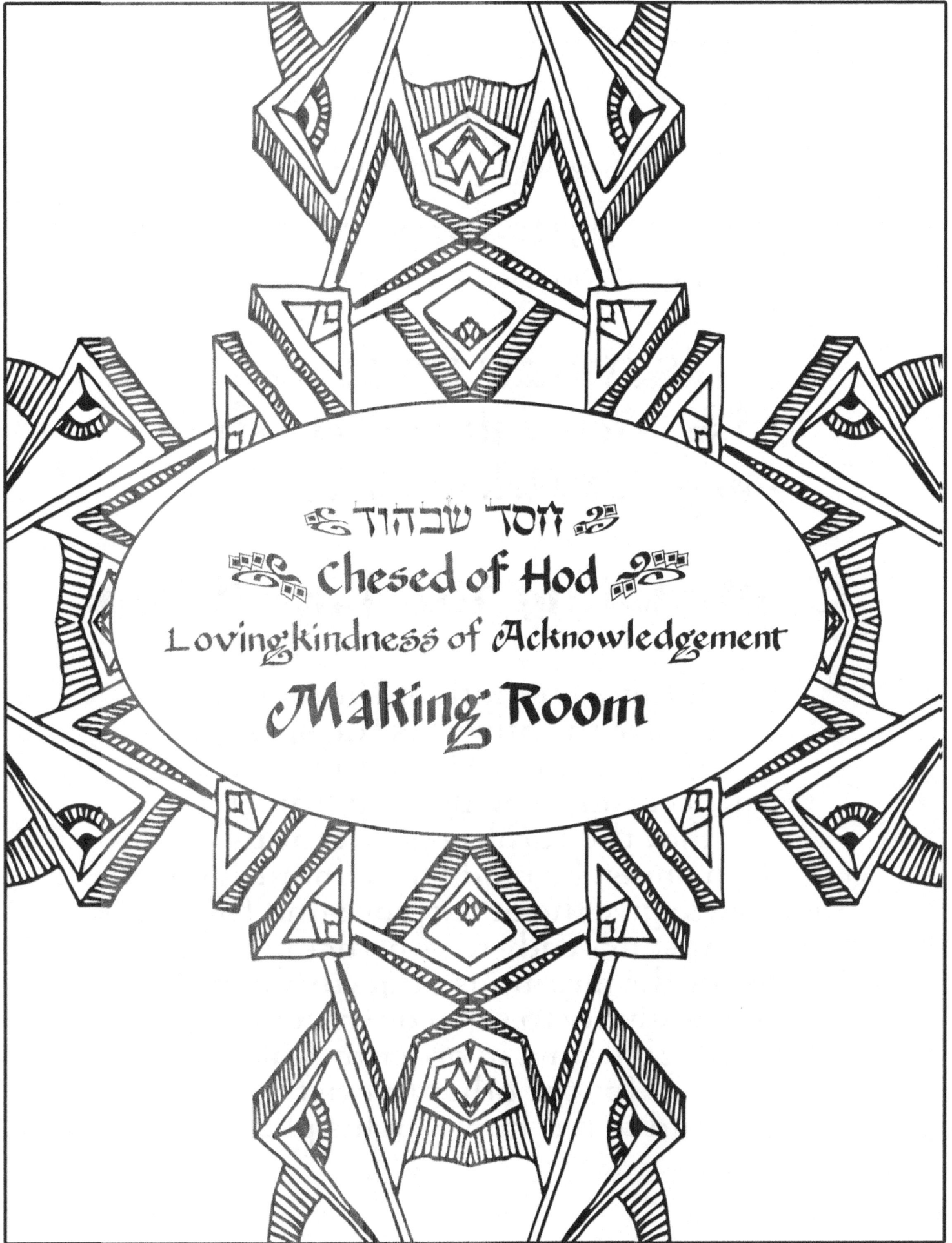

חסד שבהוד

Chesed of Hod

Lovingkindness of Acknowledgement

Making Room

Iyar 15

30 days of the Omer

הַיּוֹם שְׁלֹשִׁים יוֹם שֶׁהֵם אַרְבָּעָה שָׁבוּעוֹת וּשְׁנֵי יָמִים לָעוֹמֶר:

Today is 30 days, which is four weeks and two days of the Omer.

גבורה שבהוד
Gevurah of Hod
Might of Acknowledgement

Contracting to Make Room

It takes strength of character
to give the other his full space,
to be present, to be in that space
in accordance with the parameters
that the Torah sets out for us.
Very often I must be ready to relinquish my place,
in order to give the other place and full space.
I must be ready to contract myself.
One of the meanings of gevurah, might,
is the ability to self-contract myself,
called tzimtzum, in order to make room
for the other to exist
and to feel happy in his place.

גבורה שבהוד

Gevurah of Hod

Might of Acknowledgement

Contracting to Make Room

Iyar 16

31 days of the Omer

הַיּוֹם אֶחָד וּשְׁלשִׁים יוֹם שֶׁהֵם אַרְבָּעָה שָׁבוּעוֹת וּשְׁלשָׁה יָמִים לָעוֹמֶר:

Today is 31 days, which is four weeks and three days of the Omer.

תפארת שבהוד

Tiferet of Hod

Beauty of Acknowledgement

Aura of Splendor

Another meaning of the word Hod,
besides acknowledgement, is splendor.
Splendor is a form of beauty, tiferet,
the beauty of an acknowledgement.
A sense of beauty in splendor
is as a beautiful aura above one's head,
as a crown upon the head of a king.
When a person has true humility
and modesty, and the strength, the ability,
the conviction to give room to all others,
he merits to have an aura
of splendor above his head.
This is the beauty of acknowledgement.

תפארת שבהוד

Tiferet of Hod

Beauty of Acknowledgement

Aura of Splendor

הַיּוֹם שְׁנַיִם וּשְׁלֹשִׁים יוֹם שֶׁהֵם אַרְבָּעָה שָׁבוּעוֹת וְאַרְבָּעָה יָמִים לָעוֹמֶר:

Today is 32 days, which is four weeks and four days of the Omer.

נצח שבהוד

Netzach of Hod

Victory of Acknowledgement

Surrendering to G-d

The two powers of victory and acknowledgement act as a pair. The pair is like the game that we have discussed; there's a winner and a loser. Victory is the winner, and acknowledgement is to acknowledge that I lost.

What does it mean then that there is victory within acknowledgement? It means that there is something about losing, that the losing itself manifests winning. It's the winning of the losing, meaning that sometimes the loser, who appears to be a loser, is really the winner, That's the meaning of this sefirah of victory of acknowledgement. In which context is this meant to reflect and express itself? In the context of our relationship to G-d, to our Creator. We must surrender ourselves, surrender our will, submit ourselves to G-d's will, with the ultimate hope that His will will become our will. When we so surrender and lose to G-d, we ultimately win all. And our wills unite, and ultimately our will becomes His will and determines reality.

נצח שבהוד

Netzach of Hod

Victory of Acknowledgement

Surrendering to G‑d

LAG B'OMER

Iyar 18

33 days of the Omer

הַיּוֹם שְׁלֹשָׁה וּשְׁלשִׁים יוֹם שֶׁהֵם אַרְבָּעָה שָׁבוּעוֹת וַחֲמִשָּׁה יָמִים לָעוֹמֶר:

Today is 33 days, which is four weeks and five days of the Omer.

יסוד שבהוד
Hod of Hod
Acknowledgement of Acknowledgement

A Divine Spark

Most often, the spiritual power
of acknowledgement, hod,
is identified in Kabbalah and
Chassidut with simple, pure faith.
What is the essence of acknowledgement?
The acknowledgement of acknowledgement
is the simple faith in the absolute unity of G-d,
as well as the simple pure faith
in the spark of G-dliness
in each and every one of our souls.
The Baal Shem Tov teaches us
that just as we must believe in G-d,
so must we believe in
the Divine soul of Israel.

יסוד שבהוד

Hod of Hod

Acknowledgement of Acknowledgement

A Divine Spark

Iyar 19

34 days of the Omer

הַיוֹם אַרְבָּעָה וּשְׁלֹשִׁים יוֹם שֶׁהֵם אַרְבָּעָה שָׁבוּעוֹת וְשִׁשָּׁה יָמִים לָעוֹמֶר:

Today is 34 days, which is four weeks and six days of the Omer.

יסוד שבתפארת
Yesod of Hod
Foundation of Acknowledgement

Bonding Out of Thankfulness

The foundation of acknowledgement
is our ability to give thanks,
the spiritual attribute of thanksgiving.
There is nothing more fundamental
in a rectified personality than true thanks
to the other. By being able to express thanks,
through all of one's heart, one is able to
build a productive relationship with another.
As we have explained, yesod, foundation is
creating a covenant, a covenant of marriage
which is intended to give birth, to be productive.
Productivity begins with thanksgiving.

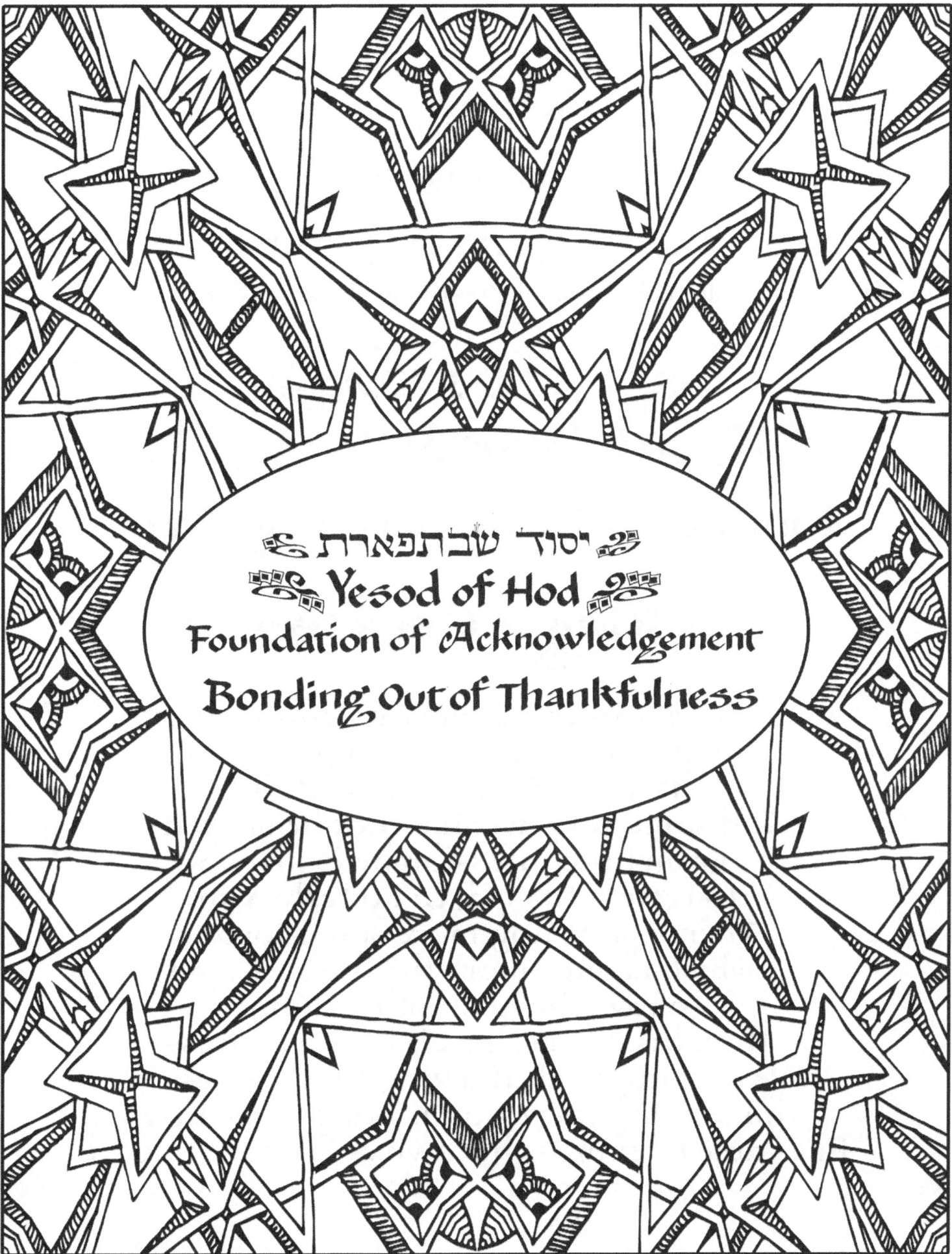

יְסוֹד שֶׁבַּתִּפְאֶרֶת

Yesod of Hod

Foundation of Acknowledgement

Bonding Out of Thankfulness

הַיּוֹם חֲמִשָּׁה וּשְׁלֹשִׁים יוֹם שֶׁהֵם חֲמִשָּׁה שָׁבוּעוֹת לָעוֹמֶר:

Today is 35 days, which is five weeks of the Omer.

מלכות שבהוד
Malchut of Hod
Kingdom of Acknowledgement

The King's Confession

There is nothing more splendorous.
Imagine a king confessing in public
that he made a mistake, that he
did something wrong, that he sinned.
From his confession he is drawn
to return to G-d, to do teshuvah.
There is nothing more splendorous,
which is once more the aura of Hod
above the head of the king,
than his power, his ability to confess.
We are taught that a king that confesses,
his whole generation is happy, because
he is able to express his own surrender to G-d.

מלכות שבהוד

Malchut of Hod

Kingdom of Acknowledgement

The King's Confession

Iyar 21

36 days of the Omer

הַיּוֹם שִׁשָּׁה וּשְׁלֹשִׁים יוֹם שֶׁהֵם חֲמִשָּׁה שָׁבוּעוֹת וְיוֹם אֶחָד לָעוֹמֶר:

Today is 36 days, which is five weeks and one day of the Omer.

חֶסֶד שֶׁבִּיסוֹד

Chesed of Yesod
Lovingkindness of Foundation

Consummation of Love

Marriage is the consummation of love.
May Hashem bless all of us that
we find our beshert, our true soulmate,
that we unite in marriage together,
that we build a home together,
that we have children together,
all in consummate love.

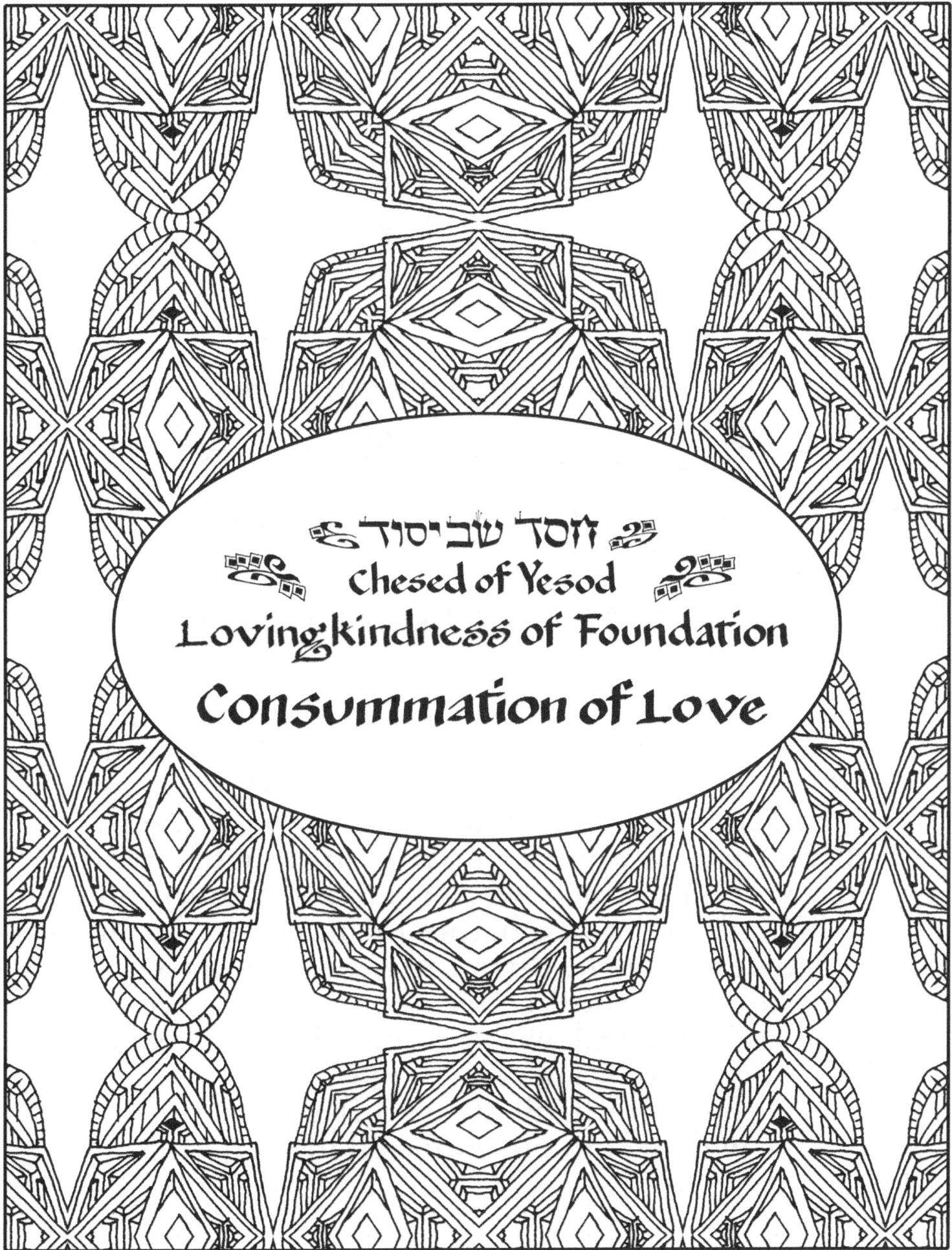

חסד שביסוד

Chesed of Yesod

Lovingkindness of Foundation

Consummation of Love

הַיּוֹם שִׁבְעָה וּשְׁלֹשִׁים יוֹם שֶׁהֵם חֲמִשָּׁה שָׁבוּעוֹת וּשְׁנֵי יָמִים לָעוֹמֶר:

Today is 37 days, which is five weeks and two days of the Omer.

גְּבוּרָה שֶׁבִּיסוֹד
Gevurah of Yesod
Might of Foundation

We Shall Overcome

When one decides to marry, one must be ready and willing to enter into a bond which entails difficulties. Not everything is smooth and easy flowing. Difficulties are misunderstandings, differences of opinion, strife. One must be ready to exert all of the power of his soul to overcome difficulties. To say, before he marries, that no matter what the difficulties are going to be, we love one another, we are creating a bond, an eternal bond, with one another, and we're going to be successful in overcoming, with strength, all of the difficulties that we will meet in our married life together.

גבורה שביסוד

Gevurah of Yesod

Might of Foundation

We Shall Overcome

Iyar 23

38 days of the Omer

הַיּוֹם שְׁמוֹנָה וּשְׁלֹשִׁים יוֹם שֶׁהֵם חֲמִשָּׁה שָׁבוּעוֹת וּשְׁלֹשָׁה יָמִים לָעוֹמֶר:

Today is 38 days, which is five weeks and three days of the Omer.

תפארת שביסוד
Tiferet of Yesod
Beauty of Foundation

The Beauty of Marriage

Under the wedding canopy,
the groom places a ring
on the finger of the bride.
The ring is a symbol of beauty,
that our marriage will be consummate,
and will be beautiful, will shine and
radiate as bright as the gold of the ring.
This is the beauty of marriage,
which begins with the marriage ceremony
under the canopy.

תפארת שביסוד

Tiferet of Yesod

Beauty of Foundation

The Beauty of Marriage

הַיּוֹם תִּשְׁעָה וּשְׁלשִׁים יוֹם שֶׁהֵם חֲמִשָּׁה שָׁבוּעוֹת וְאַרְבָּעָה יָמִים לָעוֹמֶר:

Today is 39 days, which is five weeks and four days of the Omer.

נצח שביסוד
Netzach of Yesod
Victory of Foundation

Eternal Oath

Marriage is meant to be an eternal bond.
An eternal bond means that each one of
the married couple is totally committed to
loyalty and faithfulness to his or her spouse.
This is the essence of the eternity of the
marriage. Obviously without that loyalty
and faithfulness, the marriage cannot exist,
cannot continue. The Netzach, the eternity
(which is also the victory of the foundation)
is the covenant of marriage, the pledge,
the oath of the couple under the
wedding canopy, to forever and ever
be loyal and faithful, one to the other.

נצח שביסוד

Netzach of Yesod

Victory of Foundation

Eternal Oath

הַיּוֹם אַרְבָּעִים יוֹם שֶׁהֵם חֲמִשָּׁה שָׁבוּעוֹת וַחֲמִשָּׁה יָמִים לָעוֹמֶר:

Today is 40 days, which is five weeks and five days of the Omer.

הוד שביסוד
Hod of Yesod
Acknowledgement of Foundation

Take Nothing for Granted

Very often married couples forget
to acknowledge all of the good
that their spouse does for them.
The acknowledgement and thanksgiving
within foundation is: don't forget
that the good that you receive is not automatic.
We don't really deserve it.
Everything that you receive is a gift.
Don't take for granted even the smallest
things that your spouse does.
Learn how to express thanks
from a loving heart, and in that way
the home will be full of goodness
and appreciation.

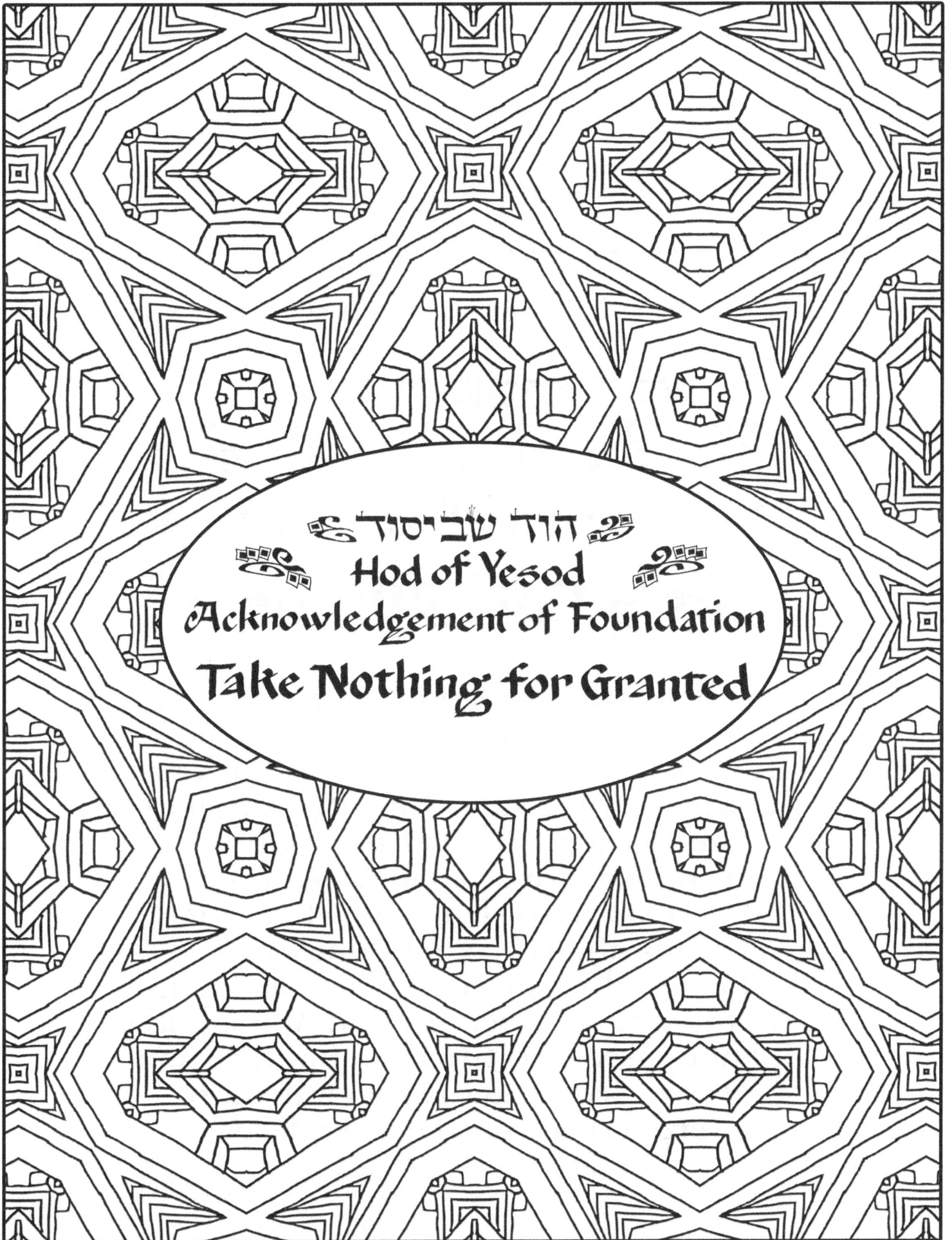

הוד שביסוד

Hod of Yesod

Acknowledgement of Foundation

Take Nothing for Granted

הַיּוֹם אֶחָד וְאַרְבָּעִים יוֹם שֶׁהֵם חֲמִשָּׁה שָׁבוּעוֹת וְשִׁשָּׁה יָמִים לָעוֹמֶר:

Today is 41 days, which is five weeks and six days of the Omer.

יסוד שביסוד
Yesod of Yesod
Foundation of Foundation

Let's Talk About It

Rectified communication
is the essence of marriage.
It's the foundation of the foundation.
In the words of the sages, marital union itself,
the physical union of the spouses,
is referred to as communication.
We must rectify, learn how to rectify
our ability to communicate.
The initial sin in the Garden of Eden,
we are taught, was because that Adam and Eve
did not possess rectified communication.
May we learn how to communicate
properly in word and in deed.

יסוד שביסוד

Yesod of Yesod

Foundation of Foundation

Let's Talk About It

Iyar 27

42 days of the Omer

הַיּוֹם שְׁנַיִם וְאַרְבָּעִים יוֹם שֶׁהֵם שִׁשָּׁה שָׁבוּעוֹת לָעוֹמֶר:

Today is 42 days, which is six weeks of the Omer.

מלכות שביסוד
Malchut of Yesod
Kingdom of Foundation

All from the Wife

There is no king without a queen.
The queen is the one who makes the king.
Not only does she make, meaning that
she properly forms the king and shapes his will,
and his ability to properly serve his people,
she also mothers the king to be.
The kingdom of marriage is that
it all depends upon the queen.
In the words of the sages,
"All is from the wife."

מלכות שביסוד

Malchut of Yesod

Kingdom of Foundation

All from the Wife

Iyar 28

43 days of the Omer

הַיּוֹם שְׁלֹשָׁה וְאַרְבָּעִים יוֹם שֶׁהֵם שִׁשָּׁה שָׁבוּעוֹת וְיוֹם אֶחָד לָעוֹמֶר:

Today is 43 days, which is six weeks and one day of the Omer.

חסד שבמלכות
Chesed of Malchut
Lovingkindness of Kingdom

Ruling Out of Good Will

Each one of us has an innate desire to lead,
a desire for kingship. That desire can be good,
or it can be not so good. There is a saying in
kabbalah, "I shall rule, I shall be a king."
When is that desire to kingship positive;
when is it negative?
It all depends on the motivation.
If the motivation is just to serve for my own
power, it's not good. But if the motivation,
the desire to be a king, is the love of the people,
the desire to do good, that the people deserve
good, that all those that I lead deserve good,
and I am the one who is able to do good to all,
then the desire is very positive.
The more the desire to do good,
the more worthy are you to be a king.

חסד שבמלכות

Chesed of Malchut

Lovingkindness of Kingdom

Ruling Out of Good Will

הַיּוֹם אַרְבָּעָה וְאַרְבָּעִים יוֹם שֶׁהֵם שִׁשָּׁה שָׁבוּעוֹת וּשְׁנֵי יָמִים לָעוֹמֶר:

Today is 44 days, which is six weeks and two days of the Omer.

גבורה שבמלכות
Gevurah of Malchut
Might of Kingdom

Focused Leadership

One of the meanings of Might,
the sefira of Gevurah, is the ability
to concentrate, to focus all of one's energy,
one's mental energy, one's emotional energy.
To focus upon a given objective, whether it's
a short-term objective, or a long-term objective.
A king, a leader, must possess the power,
the gevurah, to properly focus on the exact
needs of every individual within his domain,
to bestow upon him that which he desires.
But that demands total concentration
and focus, which is an act of might,
the might of the king.

גבורה שבמלכות

Gevurah of Malchut

Might of Kingdom

Focused Leadership

הַיּוֹם חֲמִשָּׁה וְאַרְבָּעִים יוֹם שֶׁהֵם שִׁשָּׁה שָׁבוּעוֹת וּשְׁלֹשָׁה יָמִים לָעוֹמֶר:

Today is 45 days, which is six weeks and three days of the Omer.

תפארת שבבמלכות
Tiferet of Malchut
Beauty of Kingdom

Harmonious Hierarchy

The Kingdom entails a hierarchy.
There are all levels, the head of state which is
the king himself, followed by the viceroy, and so
forth - a whole pyramid of hierarchy.
The beauty of a kingdom is when all
the levels of the hierarchy are harmonious,
they all sing together, they all interrelate.
The energy flows from the bottom of
the pyramid to the top of the pyramid,
and from the top of the pyramid
to the bottom of the pyramid,
all in beauty and harmony.
This is the beauty of kingdom.

תפארת שבמלכות

Tiferet of Malchut

Beauty of Kingdom

Harmonious Hierarchy

46 days of the Omer

הַיּוֹם שִׁשָּׁה וְאַרְבָּעִים יוֹם שֶׁהֵם שִׁשָּׁה שָׁבוּעוֹת וְאַרְבָּעָה יָמִים לָעוֹמֶר:

Today is 46 days, which is six weeks and four days of the Omer.

בצח שבמלכות
Netzach of Malchut
Victory of Kingdom

Everything Is Under Control

In all situations that present themselves
in public life, the life of kingdom,
(Kingdom can be the kingdom of the home,
of the school, of the company,
of the whole nation) in all situations,
the leader, the king, has to be in control.
He has to show his people that he is
on top of what's happening,
whether it's good or the opposite.
When the people see that the leader
is always in control, never loses control
of the situation, that's what makes them
want to be led by this leader.

נצח שבמלכות

Netzach of Malchut

Victory of Kingdom

Everything Is Under Control

Sivan 3

47 days of the Omer

הַיּוֹם שִׁבְעָה וְאַרְבָּעִים יוֹם שֶׁהֵם שִׁשָּׁה שָׁבוּעוֹת וַחֲמִשָּׁה יָמִים לָעוֹמֶר:

Today is 47 days, which is six weeks and five days of the Omer.

הוד שבבמלכות
Hod of Malchut
Acknowledgement of Kingdom
A fitting Crown

The sages say that one of the signs of a true leader is that the crown fits him, fits his head. A person who wants to rule, but is not intended by G-d to be the king of the people, the crown will not fit him. There is something in this idiom, this metaphor of the crown fitting the head, that also means that the people who have an observant eye will recognize if the position of kingship fits this particular individual. There is something that a sensitive people has with regard to the potential leader. Does kingship fit his personality? This is even without the concept of charisma, that we mentioned previously. Does kingship fit him? That acknowledgement, or realization, recognition that he is fit to be a king, is something latent in the essence of the heart of he who is intended to be. The people accept him to be the king. So may we find and recognize that individual whose kingdom fits him.

הוד שבמלכות

Hod of Malchut

Acknowledgement of Kingdom

A fitting Crown

Sivan 4

48 days of the Omer

הַיּוֹם שְׁמוֹנָה וְאַרְבָּעִים יוֹם שֶׁהֵם שִׁשָּׁה שָׁבוּעוֹת וְשִׁשָּׁה יָמִים לָעוֹמֶר:

Today is 48 days, which is six weeks and six days of the Omer.

יסוד שבבמלכות
Yesod of Malchut
Foundation of Kingdom

The King and the Teacher

One of the meanings of the sefira of yesod, foundation, is connecting oneself to the tzadik, to the most righteous individual soul of the generation. That very, very righteous tzadik of the generation is not necessarily the king of the generation. They can be two different individuals. But one of the signs of a good, and just, and true king is that he has a mentor. He has a spiritual guide, and that guide ideally should be a living soul, a living tzadik that he connects to. He is his Rebbe.

This is the yesod, the foundation of kingship, that kingship demands humility. And one of the signs of a true king is that he connects to the tzadik, to the most righteous individual of the generation, and seeks his advice and guidance.

יסוד שבמלכות
Yesod of Malchut
Foundation of Kingdom
The King and the Teacher

Sivan 5

49 days of the Omer

הַיּוֹם תִּשְׁעָה וְאַרְבָּעִים יוֹם שֶׁהֵם שִׁבְעָה שָׁבוּעוֹת לָעוֹמֶר:

Today is 49 days, which is seven weeks of the Omer.

מלכות שבבמלכות
Malchut of Malchut
Kingdom of Kingdom

The Kingdom of Heaven Within the Kingdom of Earth

We are commanded in the Torah to appoint a king. The exact phrase in the Torah reads, "Place, you shall place upon yourself a king." Why does it say "Place, you shall place" twice? The Zohar interprets it to mean that first we must place G-d as our absolute King, the King of Kings. And only then shall we place a king of flesh in our domain, in our world. What is the deep meaning of the duality of first G-d the King, and then a king, a mortal man? It means that the kingdom of earth must be totally absolutely permeated with the Kingdom of Heaven. The king in flesh must be totally nullified in his very essence to the King of Kings, to G-d. Only then will the divine, heavenly kingdom enter into his earthly kingdom, and give him the power to bring true peace and prosperity, and spiritual enlightenment to the whole world.

מלכות שבבמלכות

Malchut of Malchut

Kingdom of Kingdom

The kingdom of Heaven
Within the kingdom of Earth

Counting of the Omer
is now complete.

These meditations were inspired by video clips
from Rabbi Yitzchak Ginsburgh
available on his Youtube channel
(www.youtube.com/innerorg).
These meditations were not seen by
Rabbi Ginsburgh and the author is solely
responsible for their contents.

With profound gratitude to
Margalit & Mordechai Leaderman
Who sponsored this book,
and whose vision brought this book to life

To Rav Yitzchok Ginsburgh
Rav Yitzchok Feivsh Ben Breina Malka
May he live and be well and keep spreading
his light ever brighter to inspire and add
infinite spiritual meaning to our lives.

With gratitude to:
My dear husband Yosef Yitzchok Shagalov,
my advisor in all things

To Sterna Citron for her expert editing &
Rabbi Moshe Genuth for his guidance and
permission to bring this book to publication

10 WAYS TO BE JOYFULLY JEWISH

The most important principle in the Torah is the protection of Jewish life. It's more important than *Shabbat*, more important than holidays, even fasting on Yom Kippur. Right now, in Israel, and everywhere, Jews must stand together in unity and do whatever possible to protect Jewish life.

The Lubavitcher Rebbe, Rabbi Menachem M. Schneerson, teaches that there are **ten** important *Mitzvahs** we can do to protect life. We urgently need your help to increase in mitzvahs and merits for the Jewish people. Please choose a mitzvah to begin or improve:

1) *AHAVAS YISROEL*: Behave with love towards another Jew.

2) LEARN TORAH: Join a Torah class.

3) Make sure that Jewish children get a TORAH-TRUE EDUCATION.

4) Affix kosher *MEZUZAS* on all doorways of the house.

5) For men and boys over 13: Put on *TEFILLIN* every weekday.

6) Give CHARITY.

7) Buy JEWISH HOLY BOOKS and learn them.

8) LIGHT *SHABBAT & YOM TOV* CANDLES, a *Mitzvah* for women and girls.

9) Eat and drink only KOSHER FOOD.

10) Observe the laws of JEWISH FAMILY PURITY.

In addition the Rebbe urges that:

Every Jewish man, woman and child should have a letter written for them in a *Sefer Torah.***

Every person should study either the Rambam's *Yad Hachazakah* -- Code of Jewish Law -- or the Rambam's *Sefer HaMitzvos.*

Concerning Moshiach, the Rebbe stated, "The time for our redemption has arrived!" Everyone should prepare themselves for Moshiach's coming by doing increasing acts of goodness and kindness, and by studying about what the future redemption will be like. May we merit to see the fulfillment of the Rebbe's prophecy, Now!

----

*Mitzvahs are Divine Commandments that connect us to G-d.

**There are several Torah scrolls being written to unite Jewish people and protect Jewish life.

Letters for children can be purchased for only $1 via the Internet, at: http://www.kidstorah.org

Listen to inspiring Chassidic Torah classes while you color at Maayon.com.

For more information about how to be Joyfully Jewish, visit:

Holysparks.com	Moshiach.net	Chabad.org
Jewishwoman.org	Jewishkids.org	Maayon.com

Learn about the 7 special commandments for Righteous Gentiles:

Holysparks.com/pages/7-mitzvahs-for-non-jews

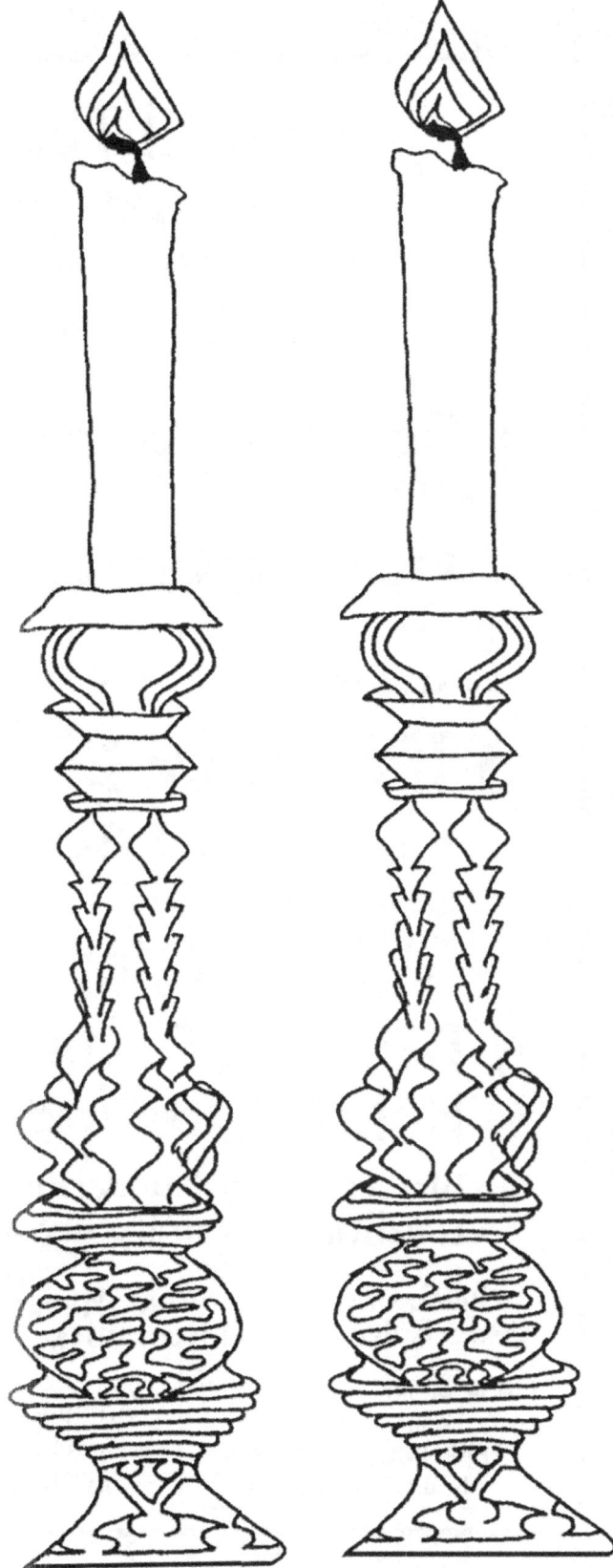

Joyfully Jewish

בָּרוּךְ אַתָּה אדנָ-י אֱ-לֹהֵינוּ מֶלֶךְ הָעוֹלָם אֲשֶׁר קִדְּשָׁנוּ בְּמִצְוֹתָיו וְצִוָּנוּ לְהַדְלִיק נֵר שֶׁל שַׁבָּת קֹדֶשׁ

TRANSLITERATION:
BARUCH A-TA A-DO-NAY
ELO-HEI-NU ME-LECH HA-O-LAM
A-SHER KI-DI-SHA-NU
BI-MITZ-VO-TAV VI-TZI-VA-NOO
LI-HAD-LEEKNER SHEL SHA-BAT
KO-DESH.

TRANSLATION:
BLESSED ARE YOU, L-RD OUR G-D,
KING OF THE UNIVERSE, WHO HAS
SANCTIFIED US WITH HIS
COMMANDMENTS, AND
COMMANDED US TO KINDLE THE
LIGHT OF THE HOLY SHABBAT.

Lighting Shabbos candles brings peace, not only to the family, lighting Shabbos candles illuminates the whole world.

~ The Zohar ~

Holy Sparks © 2019 Rae Shagalov

This coloring page is from the *Joyfully Jewish* Coloring Book available on Amazon.com
Sign up for more FREE Art & Coloring Pages
at: WWW.JOYFULLYJEWISH.COM

Enjoy coloring! But please do not color on Shabbat or other Jewish Holy Days.
The candle-lighting blessing printed here is sacred.
Please do not discard or desecrate

World Peace NOW! 7 Universal Laws for All Mankind.

The true Hope for all of humanity!

1. **Belief in G-d:** Don't worship idols

2. **Honor G-d:** Don't be disrespectful to G-d with your speech.

3. **Preserve Human Life:** Do not murder. Value the sanctity of all human lives.

4. **Respect Family Relationships:** No acts that undermine traditional family life.

The Seven Laws of Noah — G-d's Rules for All Humanity

5. **Respect other's property:** Even if times get tough, don't cheat others or steal their money or stuff.

6. **Show compassion for animals:** Don't eat meat that came from a live animal. No cruelty to animals!

7. **Establish Honest Courts:** Uphold a just legal system.

FOR MORE INFO GO TO:
ASKNOAH.ORG
LEARNMOSHIACH.COM
HOLYSPARKS.COM

Moshiach is ready to come NOW! Our part is to add in acts of goodness and kindness. ~The Lubavitcher Rebbe~

Holy Sparks

בס"ד

This Publication Is Dedicated To The Rebbe,
Rabbi Menachem M. Schneerson of Lubavitch

whose teachings and inspiration lives in us, and fires us up
to try and reach heights we can't reach on our own,
to prepare the whole world for the imminent arrival of Moshiach.

IN LOVING MEMORY OF

Harav Schneur Zalman Halevi ע"ה
ben Harav Yitzchok Elchonon Halevi הי"ד Shagalov

Reb Dovid Asniel ben Reb Eliyahu ע"ה

Devora Rivka bas Reb Yosef Eliezer ע"ה

Reb Yitzchok Moshe ben Reb Dovid Asniel ע"ה

❧   May Their Souls Merit Eternal Life   ☙

AND IN HONOR OF

Mrs. Esther Shaindel bas Fraidel Chedva שתחי' Shagalov
and Our Dear Children and Grandchildren שיחיו
May You Always Be Joyfully Jewish!

DEDICATED BY

Rabbi & Mrs. Yosef Yitzchok and Gittel Rachel שיחיו Shagalov

To dedicate future editions in
honor or memory of your
loved ones, contact us at:
info@holysparks.com

❧ABOUT HOLY SPARKS❧

Holy Sparks is dedicated to spreading the light of authentic Jewish spirituality and wisdom through Jewish education with creative expression. Holy Sparks provides and promotes Jewish knowledge, awareness and practice as it applies to people of all faiths and nationalities, regardless of affiliation or background. Holy Sparks helps spiritual seekers, particularly the Jewish people, and others who are looking for inspiration and encouragement, to discover and fulfill their individual talents and potential for serving G-d and mankind through increasing acts of goodness, kindness, and holiness.

❧ABOUT RAE SHAGALOV❧

Master calligrapher Rae Shagalov is the author of the Amazon bestseller, "The Secret Art of Talking to G-d" and the "Joyfully Jewish" series of interactive calligraphy and coloring books for adults and families. Rae is eager to share the beauty and wisdom of Torah through her 3,000 pages of beautifully designed Artnotes that reveal the special message of this exciting time in Jewish History. Rae has combined her experience as a creativity coach, her talent as a Jewish artist, and her fascinating spiritual search for the true meaning of life to produce these beautiful Jewish Artnotes and books. Rae's books provide her readers with very practical, joy-based action steps for infusing authentic Jewish spirituality into their daily lives. Rae offers Creative Clarity Coaching for women who want to use their creativity, discover their Life Purpose and elevate their spiritual growth through the deep wisdom and secrets of the Torah. Find out more about Rae Shagalov's Passion Projects Mastermind, coaching & workshops at: www.CreativeJewishSoul.com.

❧ CONNECT WITH RAE ❧

Sign up to receive free art, coloring pages
and Rae's Soul Tips newsletter!
Go to: www.holysparks.com

LET'S CONNECT!

Facebook.com/soultips
Pinterest.com/holysparks
Twitter.com/holysparks
Youtube.com/holysparksbooks

There's a Holy Spark in each of us
that's hidden very well;
when it's revealed, we make our world
a place where G-d can dwell.

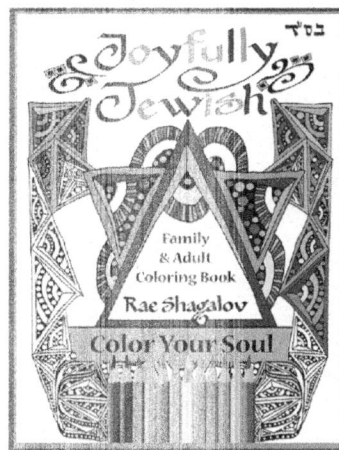

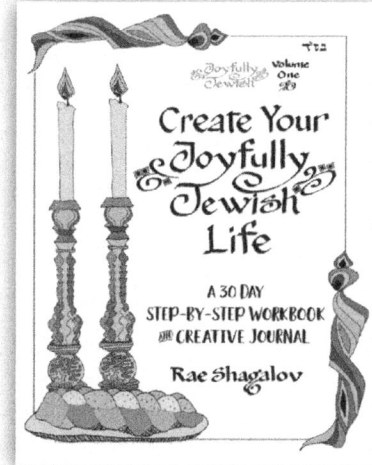

NOTES

NOTES

NOTES

NOTES

NOTES